FREDDIE MERCURY

ANNE COLLINS

LEVEL

SERIES EDITOR: SORREL PITTS

Many of the quotes in this book have been simplified
for learners of English as a foreign language.

PENGUIN BOOKS

UK | USA | Canada | Ireland | Australia
India | New Zealand | South Africa

Penguin Books is part of the Penguin Random House group of companies
whose addresses can be found at global.penguinrandomhouse.com.
www.penguin.co.uk www.puffin.co.uk www.ladybird.co.uk

First published 2020

001

Text written by Anne Collins
Text copyright © Penguin Books Ltd, 2020
Cover design by Guy Harvey

Photo credits:
Cover and page 6 (Freddie Mercury at Live Aid Concert) © Popperfoto/Getty Images.co.uk; page 11 © Stringer/
AFP/Getty Images.co.uk; page 12 (blue plaque) © Mick Sinclair/Alamy Stock Photo; page 12 (Freddie's first
home) © Benjamin John/Alamy Stock Photo; page 13 © Pictorial Press Ltd/Alamy Stock Photo; page 17 ©
Marc Sharratt/Shutterstock; pages 19 and 21 © Michael Putland/Getty Images; page 24 © Monitor Picture
Library/Photoshot/Getty Images; page 26 © Ilpo Musto/Shutterstock; page 27 © GAB Archive/Redferns/
Getty Images; page 30 © Anwar Hussein/Getty Images; page 36 © Koh Hasebe/Shinko Music/Getty Images;
page 43 © Keystone Features/Getty Images; pages 50 and 70 © Dave Hogan/Hulton Archive/Getty Images;
page 54 © Siemoneit/ullstein bild/Getty Images; pages 57 and 58 © Photoshot/TopFoto; page 61 © PA
Photos/TopFoto; page 64 © akg-images/picture-alliance/dpa; page 65 © Picture Alliance/Bridgeman Images;
page 66 © FG/Bauer-Griffin/Getty Images; page 73 © Richard Young/Shutterstock; page 78 © Shutterstock;
page 79 © Arnold Slater/Mirrorpix/Getty Images; pages 80-81 © Phil Dent/Redferns/Getty Images.

Printed in China

A CIP catalogue record for this book is available from the British Library

ISBN: 978-0-241-43098-9

All correspondence to
Penguin Random House Children's
One Embassy Gardens, New Union Square
5 Nine Elms Lane, London SW8 5DA

Contents

Note about the book	4
Before-reading questions	5
Chapter One – The boy from Zanzibar	7
Chapter Two – The birth of Queen	14
Chapter Three – Friends and lovers	22
Chapter Four – First steps to success	28
Chapter Five – Queen at number one	35
Chapter Six – Having a good time	42
Chapter Seven – From rock to disco	48
Chapter Eight – The end of Queen?	56
Chapter Nine – "We Are the Champions"	62
Chapter Ten – The last years	71
During-reading questions	84
After-reading questions	86
Exercises	87
Project work	91
Glossary	92
References	96
Bibliography	96

Note about the book

In 1964, Farrokh Bulsara, a shy young boy from Zanzibar, arrived in London with his parents and sister to escape a **revolution*** and follow his dream of becoming a **rock star**. As Farrokh soon discovered, London in the 1960s was an exciting time when anything seemed possible for young people. It was not long before Farrokh had met three other **talented** young **musicians**, and together they **formed** the band Queen. But the road to success was not an easy one. Many things changed for Farrokh as he became Freddie Mercury, one of the greatest rock stars of all time. As Queen became more and more famous all over the world, it seemed that nothing could stop them. But then problems started to appear, **including** a strange and terrible illness that changed everything not only for Freddie but also for Queen, and for the other people whom Freddie loved best.

*Definitions of words in **bold** can be found in the glossary on pages 92–95.

Note: There are some above-level words in the titles of songs and **albums** that do not appear in the glossary.

Some of the sentences in this book have been taken from other books. Each of those sentences has a number after it. The references on page 96 tell you which other books those sentences come from.

Before-reading questions

1 Look at the cover of the book, and read the title. Describe the man. Do you know his real name? What other things do you know about him? Think about:
   a when and where he was born
   b how he died
   c why he was famous.

2 What do you know about the rock band Queen? For example, do you know:
   a when the band started
   b who was in the band
   c what they did in the band
   d the names of some of Queen's most famous songs?

3 What are the good things and the difficult things about being famous, do you think? How can becoming famous change someone's life? Would you like to be famous? Why/Why not? Give your reasons.

4 Think of some other great singers and musicians. What special abilities do they have? What makes them different from other people?

Freddie at Live Aid concert in 1985

CHAPTER ONE
The boy from Zanzibar

It was Wednesday 5th September 2018, another normal day at London's busy Heathrow Airport. Passengers who had just arrived at the British Airways building stood waiting to collect their bags. Some were looking at their phones, while others talked quietly to their friends. Nobody had any idea that something amazing was going to happen.

Suddenly the music of "I Want to Break Free", a song by the famous **rock** band Queen, started playing loudly. Immediately a group of airport workers stopped work and started dancing to the music. Each man was dressed like Queen's **lead** singer, Freddie Mercury. They wore white trousers and bright yellow jackets, and each had a big, black moustache. They danced around small yellow or white cases. The people watching were very surprised. They looked at the men, and then they looked at each other and began to smile. Some began taking videos on their phones, while others started moving to the music. Everybody felt happy as they watched the men dancing.

The airport workers had worked hard for weeks, practising their dance. Although Freddie had been dead for many years, he was born on 5th September 1946, and they wanted to remember his birthday. Not many people knew that, before he became a famous rock **star**, Freddie had worked at Heathrow Airport for a short time. There were several other surprises for passengers that day. The names of famous Queen songs appeared on information boards, and people called Freddie, Frederick or Farrokh (Freddie Mercury's real name) were invited by British Airways to use their lounge for free. It was a wonderful way to remember a great rock star.

Freddie had died in November 1991, but people all over the world still loved his music, and Queen's songs were famous in many different countries. A movie about the story of Freddie and Queen, *Bohemian Rhapsody*, was going to be **released** in October 2018. Most people knew that Freddie Mercury was an amazing songwriter and **musician**. But they did not know much about his life, or that Freddie's story started in a very different country from the United Kingdom.

Freddie's life story is very interesting, and it began far away from the UK, in Stone Town on the island of Zanzibar. His father, Bomi Bulsara, had travelled to Zanzibar from India several years before to work. The British had controlled Zanzibar since 1890, and Bomi had a good job working for the British **government**. However, he often had to go back to India on business, and, on one of these visits, he met and fell in love with a girl called Jer, who was fourteen years younger than him.

Bomi and Jer married, and Jer went to Zanzibar to start

a new life with her husband. Their first child, Farrokh, was born on 5th September 1946, and six years later they had a daughter, Kashmira.

Little Farrokh was a good-looking child, and when he was six months old he won first **prize** in a competition for the most beautiful baby. By the age of four or five, he loved singing at the parties of his parents and their friends. As a small child, he went to school in Zanzibar, but in 1955 his parents decided to send him to India to St Peter's School in Panchgani, which is south east of Mumbai. The school was almost 3,000 miles from Zanzibar, so, for the next few years, Farrokh could only go home and see his family for one month each year in the summer holidays. During his first years at St Peter's School, he was very quiet. He was **especially** shy about his teeth because he had four extra teeth at the back of his mouth, and this made him look different from the other boys. He was very good at sports, music and art, and when he was eleven he won an important prize for sport. Some of the teachers and other students at the school called him "Freddie" instead of "Farrokh". He liked this name very much, and he started calling himself Freddie Bulsara.

Freddie had always loved music, but in Zanzibar he had mostly listened to Indian music. However, at St Peter's he became very interested in **Western** pop music, and in 1958, at the age of twelve, he **formed** his first band with four schoolfriends. They called themselves The Hectics, and they played rock music. They wore white shirts and black ties.

Freddie was having piano lessons, so he became the band's piano player. He had a special ability, because as soon as he had heard a song once on the radio he was able to play it on the piano. The Hectics often played at the school and also became very **popular** with the people in the town, especially the girls!

However, The Hectics came to an end on 25th February 1963, when Freddie left St Peter's and went back to Zanzibar to live with his family. Western music and fashions were still very important to him, and, when he could, he read Western magazines. He dreamed of going to live in the West, but he did not know how he was going to do that.

Then something happened in Zanzibar that changed the lives of thousands of people, **including** Freddie's family. Over the centuries, many different groups of people from many countries in Africa and Asia had come to live in Zanzibar. Until December 1963, the British had controlled Zanzibar, but then a new government was formed by the Zanzibar National Party (ZNP). However, other groups were against the new government, and one month later a **revolution** started. It moved quickly across Zanzibar towards Stone Town, and thousands of Arabs and Indians were killed. Things were becoming very dangerous for ordinary people, and the Bulsaras and many other families were frightened for their children. So the Bulsaras decided to leave as quickly as possible, taking only a few things with them. Freddie's father, Bomi, had worked for

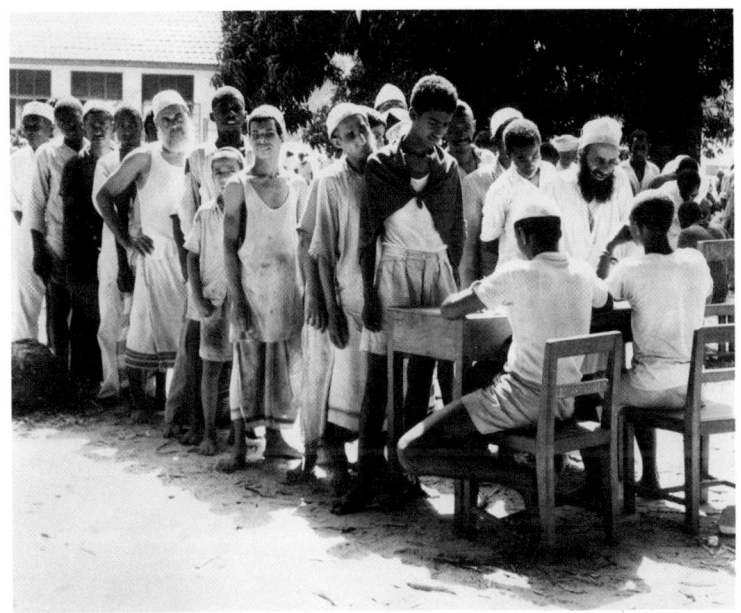

Arabs being questioned during the Zanzibar Revolution

the British government in Zanzibar, so the family decided not to go back to India but to start a new life in the UK.

In autumn 1964, the Bulsaras moved into a house with four bedrooms at 22 Gladstone Avenue, Feltham, in southwest London, not far from Heathrow Airport. Freddie's first home in London was an ordinary house in an ordinary street. It was very different from the expensive houses where he lived after he became famous. In 2016, a blue sign was put on the wall to mark Freddie's first house in England.

Although the Bulsaras were safe in the UK, at first things were not easy for them. The colours and sounds of London were very different from those of Zanzibar.

Zanzibar had beautiful beaches, blue skies and warm days, but the skies of London were often grey and rainy. The houses, streets and shops were all very new and strange. Planes flew above the family's home on their way to and from Heathrow, making a lot of noise. Everything in London was expensive, too. In Zanzibar, Bomi had had a good job, so his family enjoyed a comfortable life. Like other families with money in Zanzibar, the Bulsaras had owned a car, and Jer had someone to help her in the house. But in London both Freddie's parents had to go out to work to **support** their family. However, Freddie was very happy to be in London because it was the start of his dream.

Freddie's first home in London

Freddie did not know that another **teenager** who loved music was living in Feltham just a few streets away. This young man's name was Brian May, and he was going to become very important in Freddie's life as the lead guitar player for Queen. Brian was studying at Imperial College, London, but he was very interested in rock music and loved

Brian playing the Red Special

playing the guitar. However, he was still a student and did not have enough money to afford his own guitar, so his dad helped him to build one. Brian called his guitar the "Red Special" because of its colour, and he played it in Queen **concerts** for many years.

CHAPTER TWO
The birth of Queen

Freddie had arrived in London at a very exciting time. His family had left Zanzibar to escape from a revolution, but a revolution was happening in Britain, too. However, this revolution was not dangerous. It was a revolution in music, fashion, film and art, and its centre was London. Suddenly London was "the place to be". On 15th April 1966, a story about London appeared in the American magazine *Time*. It called London "the Swinging City". "Swinging" means "fun and exciting", and many people remember the 1960s as "the Swinging Sixties". These years were a great time to be alive, especially for young people. They were free to enjoy themselves, and to explore new experiences. Many parents of young British people in the 1960s had not had much fun when they were young because during those years Britain was fighting in the Second World War (1939–1945). But, by the 1960s, life was good again, and for their children anything seemed possible.

London was like a wonderful dream for Freddie. For one thing, there were so many exciting new fashions. The most popular shopping areas for clothes in London were the King's Road, Kensington and Carnaby Street. Many fashion **designers** came to London, bringing new ideas with them, and they opened boutiques. These were small shops that sold clothes in the latest fashion.

Music was very important for young people in the Swinging Sixties. At that time, there were no home computers or mobile phones. But many teenagers owned a new kind of small, light radio called a transistor. Transistor radios could easily be carried around, so young people could listen to their favourite pop songs while moving from one place to another. Many new pop and rock bands were starting, like The Beatles, The Rolling Stones and The Who. On 1st January 1964, the British Broadcasting Corporation (BBC) started a new weekly TV pop-music programme called *Top of the Pops*. The first show was **broadcast** on 1st January 1964 with The Beatles as guests, **performing** their **number-one hit single**, "I Want to Hold Your Hand".

Top of the Pops quickly became very popular and was watched by young people all over Britain every week. Until 1968 it was broadcast in black and white, but in 1969 it was broadcast in colour for the first time. Top bands and singers were invited to the *Top of the Pops* **studio** to perform in front of a **live audience**. Many bands and singers wanted to appear on the show because it was a great way to **promote** their latest songs. People could also listen to their favourite pop songs on "pirate" radio **stations** like Radio Caroline and Radio London. These stations were called "pirate stations" because they were not allowed by law to broadcast in Britain, so they broadcast from ships in **international** waters.

The new music, fashion, dance and art had a strong **influence** on Freddie. He grew his hair long and started wearing clothes in the latest fashion. He was developing his own ideas about his future, which were very different from his parents' ideas. They wanted him to have a job like an accountant or a **lawyer**, but Freddie did not share their dreams. He was going to become a rock star! But first he wanted to go to art college because many famous rock stars had studied art before they became musicians. From 1964 to 1966, he went to a college in Isleworth, and then in September 1966 he started a course at Ealing School of Art, training to be a fashion designer. Freddie was making lots of new friends, but he wanted to follow his dream of being a musician, and he knew that he had to meet more people in the world of music.

On 16th December 1966, Freddie watched a BBC TV show of the first British television **performance** by Jimi Hendrix, the famous American rock guitar player, singer and songwriter. Hendrix had arrived in London in September 1966 and quickly became very popular. Soon the pirate radio stations were playing his hit single, "Hey Joe", all the time. Freddie loved everything about Hendrix – his music, clothes and hair – and he wanted to be just like him. He discovered all the places where Hendrix was playing live, and he went to see him fourteen times.

Freddie drew pictures of Jimi Hendrix and put them on his bedroom walls. He was also writing songs at home and putting them under his **pillow**. In a film called *Freddie*

THE BIRTH OF QUEEN

Jimi Hendrix in concert

Mercury: The Untold Story (2000) about Freddie's life, his mother Jer said that she often told Freddie to clean his room and throw away all the papers under his pillow. Freddie's parents were worried he was writing music instead of studying. They did not understand what their son wanted to do with his life.

But Freddie knew **exactly** what he wanted to do. He was thinking all the time about how he could become a musician. He started a different course at Ealing School of Art and made friends with another student on his new course, Tim Staffell. Tim was also very interested in music and was the singer in a band. The lead guitar player of the band was Brian May, the teenager who lived a few streets away from Freddie in Feltham. In the autumn of 1968, Tim and Brian decided to form a new band, but they needed a **drummer**. So they advertised on a board at Imperial College, London, where Brian was a student. A young drummer from Cornwall called Roger Taylor, who was also a student, heard that they were advertising and contacted Tim and Brian. The three students formed a band that they called Smile. They studied during the day but met as often as they could to talk about music and **rehearse** songs. They started writing their own songs, and they played for the first time at a **gig** at Imperial College on 26th October 1968.

Freddie and Tim were good friends, so one day Tim introduced Freddie to Brian and Roger. Freddie liked them very much and was very interested in their new band.

He became good friends with them and began spending a lot of time at Roger's flat. By this time, Freddie had left Ealing College, but he still did not have a real job. So he and Roger started selling clothes in the latest fashion at Kensington Market. Smile were playing at gigs in different places in London and Cornwall, and Freddie often went with them.

Roger Taylor

He loved listening to their music and enjoyed watching them rehearse. He wanted to be part of Smile, but they already had Tim Staffell as their singer, and they did not need Freddie. However, a band from Liverpool called Ibex were looking for a singer and asked Freddie to join them. He performed live on stage with Ibex for the first time on 23rd August 1969, singing "Jailhouse Rock" by the famous American singer Elvis Presley.

Ibex did not get the chance to play at many gigs in London, so they often played at gigs in Liverpool instead. Freddie was getting a lot of good experience with Ibex, and he was learning many things about how to perform on stage. But it was a long way from London to Liverpool, and he was getting tired of travelling from one city to the other. London was the centre of rock music, and that was where Freddie wanted to be. He left Ibex and joined another band, but it did not last for very long, and, in the spring of 1970, Freddie did not have a band. Was this the end of all his plans to be a rock star? Then suddenly he had a lucky chance. Tim Staffell decided to leave Smile because he wanted to join another band, so Brian and Roger asked Freddie to be Smile's lead singer. At last, at the age of twenty-three, it seemed that Freddie's dream had a chance of becoming real.

Roger Taylor's mother helped to **organize** a gig for Smile on 27th June 1970 in Cornwall. This was the first time that Smile had played before a live audience with Freddie as the singer. It was not a great success, but it was very good experience, and they were paid a little money. All the **members** of the band had long hair and wore black T-shirts, black trousers and high boots, with silver necklaces and rings. There were only a few people in the audience, and some of them thought the band looked very strange and their music was too loud. The band's next performance was back in London at Imperial College on 18th July 1970. This was just a small gig for a few friends.

But before then, two important changes happened. The first was that Smile had changed their name to Queen. The new name was Freddie's idea, because it was strong and **royal**, and at first Roger and Brian did not like it, but later they agreed to it. The other big change was that, in the summer of 1970, Freddie changed his name, too. He had written a song with the word "mercury" in it, and he decided to call himself Freddie Mercury.

Another important change for the band happened a few months later. They had tried different **bass** guitar players, but they had not been able to find the right person. But, in February 1971, they met a student called John Deacon who played bass guitar, and after hearing him play they realized he had a special ability. So they invited John to join them, and he became the fourth member of the new band Queen. They had no idea back then that they were going to stay together for many years and become famous all over the world.

John Deacon

CHAPTER THREE
Friends and lovers

In 1964, in the middle of the Swinging Sixties, a new boutique called Biba opened in Kensington. It was owned by the fashion designer Barbara Hulanicki. Barbara's family were from Poland, but they had moved to London after the Second World War. In the early 1960s, Barbara had studied fashion at Brighton College of Art and started making clothes, including a pink dress that became very popular and was bought by about 17,000 young women.

Biba had opened at just the right time and quickly became very popular. Many of its customers were rock stars, actors and famous people on TV. But you did not have to be famous to go shopping in Biba. The prices were not high, so students and young working women could afford to buy clothes there, too. Many young women from outside London went to the city for the day just to go shopping in Biba. They loved the short, bright dresses, skirts, trousers, T-shirts, high boots and wonderful big hats. Suddenly everybody wanted to own something from Biba, and it quickly became "the place to be".

As you walked along the street, you could hear pop music from Biba playing loudly. The people who worked there were young and friendly, and they wore clothes in the latest fashion. One of them was a beautiful nineteen-year-old girl with blonde hair and blue eyes called Mary Austin.

One evening, Brian May was at a concert at Imperial College, and Mary was sitting behind him in the audience. They started talking, and Brian asked Mary to go out with him on a **date**. Although they went out several times together as friends, their **relationship** was never very serious. However, Brian noticed that Freddie had seen Mary and was becoming very interested in her. Freddie often talked about Mary, so Brian introduced Freddie to her.

Freddie and Roger were still selling clothes in Kensington Market. So Freddie often came to Kensington, and it was easy for him to visit Biba to say hello to Mary. But he was very shy, and it took a long time for him to ask her to go out on a date. In *The Freddie Mercury: The Untold Story* (2000), Mary said, "Sometimes he was brave enough to come into the shop on his own, but mostly he came with Roger or somebody . . . This went on for five or six months. Finally, he asked me to go out on a date."[1]

Freddie first asked Mary to go out with him on 5th September, his 24th birthday, but she said no. However, he kept asking her, and a few weeks later she agreed. On their first date, they went to a rock concert. About five months later, they began living together in a flat at 2 Victoria Road, Kensington, with their two cats, Tom and Jerry. They did not have much money, so their flat was very small, and they shared a kitchen and bathroom with two other people. But they had a strong, loving relationship, and they were very happy together.

Freddie with Mary Austin

Mary did not fall in love with Freddie immediately. "It took a long while for me to really fall in love with this man. But . . . I could never turn away from him. His pain became my pain. His happiness became my happiness."[2] Freddie and Mary continued living together for six years, and the first four years were very happy. But, for the last two years, Mary knew that something had changed in their relationship. Freddie was not as relaxed or happy as he had been, and she did not know the reason.

At first, she thought he was seeing another woman, but she also thought that perhaps he was **gay**. Later, in *Freddie Mercury: The Untold Story* (2000), Mary said, "I could see that he was feeling bad about something, wasn't feeling comfortable."[3] Then one night, during a conversation in the kitchen, Freddie told Mary he thought he was **bisexual**.

In the 1950s and early 1960s, it was very difficult for bisexual and gay people in the UK to be honest about their **sexuality**. They often had to keep it a secret. It was a crime for a man to be gay, and some gay men had gone to prison. Many men had to **pretend** that they were not gay. However, on 27th July 1967 a new law was passed by the British government. After this, it was not against the law for two men to have sex privately. But, even after the 1967 law, it was still not easy to say that you were gay, because many people thought that it was wrong, and some people even believed that being gay was a kind of illness.

In Queen's early years, many people did not know the truth about Freddie's sexuality. When they saw him

FREDDIE MERCURY

performing on stage, they did not think he was gay or bisexual.

In the early 1970s, a new kind of music called glam rock was becoming very popular. Glam-rock stars mostly had long hair, dressed in women's clothes and wore lots of **make-up**. Freddie loved glam rock because he could

David Bowie

experiment with how he looked on stage. Marc Bolan and his band T. Rex were some of the first glam-rock musicians to appear on *Top of the Pops* in 1971 with their hit song "Get It On". Over the next few years, they were followed by other famous glam-rock bands and singers, like Alice Cooper, The Sweet, David Bowie, Slade and Queen.

Slade

When Freddie told Mary that he was bisexual, he was probably worried that she would be shocked and not want to support him. But Mary was pleased that Freddie had been honest with her, especially as after their conversation he became much happier and relaxed. Although they were not lovers any more, they continued to live near each other, saw each other often and stayed great friends for the rest of Freddie's life. Many people believe that Freddie wrote the song "Love of My Life" for Mary.

CHAPTER FOUR
First steps to success

Queen had four excellent musicians: a lead singer (Freddie Mercury), a lead guitar player (Brian May), a bass guitar player (John Deacon) and a drummer (Roger Taylor). Freddie was sure that, one day, Queen would be a big success. However, he was also worried because he did not have a real job, and his only money came from selling clothes in Kensington Market. He knew that Queen had to make a **deal** with a **record** company as quickly as possible. But this was not easy, because many other bands and singers were trying to do the same thing.

Bands needed record companies to help them become famous by promoting their songs and **albums** on TV and radio. Record companies needed new bands and singers, but they only made deals with **talented** artists who would sell a lot of records. Queen made a record of a song that Brian May had written called "Keep Yourself Alive". They took it to several record companies, but they did not get a record deal. So Queen continued playing gigs sometimes, and Freddie continued working at Kensington Market. By this time, the rest of Queen had finished studying, but, like Freddie, they did not want normal jobs. They wanted to make money from playing music.

Then something happened that helped Queen a lot. In March 1968, two brothers, Norman and Barry Sheffield, opened Trident Studios, a recording studio in Soho, in the centre of London. Trident Studios had excellent **equipment**, and famous bands and singers like The Beatles and David Bowie made recordings there. One night, Barry Sheffield saw Queen playing at a hospital dance, and he liked their sound very much. He told Norman about this interesting new band, and the two brothers invited Queen to their studios to talk about their future. Norman quickly realized that Freddie was a very talented young man. His voice was amazing, because he could easily sing very high and very low.

However, Queen were a new band, and Norman had only heard a few of their songs. He wanted to see what other songs they could do. So the Sheffield brothers made a deal with Queen – that Queen could use Trident's recording studios for free, and they would record new songs that Trident could promote to the record companies. Trident also agreed to buy some new equipment for Roger, and some other things that Queen needed.

This was a great chance for Queen, and, at first, they were very pleased. But there was a problem, because the recording studios were often used by other bands during the day, and the studios only became free late at night. Sometimes Queen had to wait until 2 a.m. before they could start work. Then they worked all night until the cleaners came in at 7 a.m. the next morning.

FREDDIE MERCURY

**The young members of Queen:
Brian May, Roger Taylor, John Deacon, Freddie Mercury**

In a book that he wrote later in his life, *Life on Two Legs*, Norman Sheffield remembers that all the members of the band were very different. They did not always agree with each other, and they often argued and shouted. Sometimes they even threw plates and glasses at each other, and they did not talk to each other for a few days. But their problems with each other never lasted, because they all shared the same hopes and dreams. Their music was the most important thing for all of them, and they wanted it to be excellent.

In June 1972, Norman asked Jack Nelson, an American friend of his, to be Queen's manager. Queen were very pleased about this, and Jack immediately started going round the big record companies, trying to get Queen a recording deal. Queen were writing a lot of new songs, but none of the big record companies were interested. By the end of 1972, they had recorded their first album, which they also called *Queen*, but they still could not get a deal with a record company.

However, at the start of 1973, they had a lucky chance. Trident made a deal with the BBC for Queen to record four songs at the BBC studios for a radio show called *Sounds of the Seventies*. Queen were not paid for this, but the show was very popular, and many people listened to it every week. Roy Featherstone, one of the top people at EMI, a famous record company, heard Queen on *Sounds of the Seventies*, and he immediately decided to make a deal with them. So, finally, Queen got what they had always wanted – a deal with a top record company.

In August 1973, Queen started recording their second album, *Queen II*, with eleven songs. Six of them were written by Freddie. Norman and Jack decided that it was time for Queen to do a live **tour** to promote their music. So for the rest of the year Queen played at different gigs around the UK. At the same time, they were hoping for a hit single in the music **charts**. In January 1974, they were invited to Australia to play as the top band in a concert. But things did not go very well for them there. Brian was ill, Freddie had a problem with his ear and there were also problems with the band's equipment. Also, some people were angry because Queen were not yet famous, and they could not understand why Queen were the top band instead of an Australian band. So Queen decided to come back to London early, but, before they left, Freddie told the crowds, "When Queen come back to Australia, we will be the biggest band in the world."

Soon after Queen arrived back in London, something very exciting happened. David Bowie, the famous glam-rock singer, was invited to perform on *Top of the Pops* on 21st February 1974. But, two days before, he suddenly had to **cancel**, and Robin Nash, who organized the show, had to find another band or singer very quickly. He asked EMI to help him find a band who could perform instead of Bowie. EMI sent a record of Queen's songs to Nash, and he liked their music and asked them to appear on the show. At that time, the weekly audience of *Top of the Pops* was about 15 million people, so this was an excellent way for Queen to promote their music. The show was recorded on 20th February, and Queen played a song from their second album called "Seven Seas of Rhye", which Freddie had written. However, none of the band owned a TV. So, when the show was broadcast the next evening, they had to go to a shop that sold TVs and watch themselves on *Top of the Pops* through the shop window!

Two days later, EMI made a single of "Seven Seas of Rhye", which reached number ten in the UK's Top Ten singles charts. This song was Queen's first hit single, and it stayed in the charts for several weeks. Until the success of "Seven Seas of Rhye", Freddie was still working in Kensington Market. But, after the song became a **hit**, Freddie and the other band members decided to give all their time to Queen. Queen's second album, *Queen II*, was released and reached number five in the UK album charts. As everything seemed to be going well for the band, Trident decided to organize a tour of the United States of America for them. But, although the tour began well, later things started to go wrong. After only twenty gigs, Brian became seriously ill and was flown back to the UK. Queen could not continue without him, so they had to cancel the rest of the tour, which meant that Queen and Trident lost money. Brian was in hospital for six weeks, while Freddie, Roger and John started writing songs for their third album, *Sheer Heart Attack*. Freddie wrote six of the songs on the new album, including Queen's next big hit, "Killer Queen", which was very different to the loud rock music of many of their other songs.

When bands release a new album, they choose one or two of its best songs to release as single records, or "singles". "Killer Queen" was released as a single on 21st October 1974 and reached number two in the UK singles charts, while *Sheer Heart Attack* reached number two in the

UK album charts. The popular British radio **disc jockey** (DJ) Kenny Everett helped Queen a lot by promoting "Killer Queen" and *Sheer Heart Attack*. Kenny had worked on pirate radio stations in the 1960s before joining BBC Radio One in 1967. By 1974, he had his own breakfast show on Capital Radio in London, which millions of people listened to. Like Freddie, Everett was very **flamboyant**. He loved Queen's music, and, one morning in 1974, he invited Freddie to be a guest on his show. After that, Freddie and Kenny became good friends, and Kenny often played Queen's songs.

CHAPTER FIVE
Queen at number one

Queen were becoming famous, not only in the UK but in other countries in Europe as well. They went on another British tour and also performed at gigs in Sweden, Finland, Germany, Holland, Belgium and Spain. At every gig, Freddie was the star of the show. He loved performing live and always did his best to make his audience happy. Next, Trident organized a big international tour for the band.

In January 1975, they went back to the USA again. Everything started well, but then Freddie started having problems with his voice. He went to see a doctor, who told him he should not sing for the next three months. Queen had a concert in Washington that evening, and Freddie was very worried because he did not want to cancel it. He continued with the show, but Jack Nelson cancelled some of Queen's other concerts. By the end of the tour, Queen had played at only thirty-three out of the forty-eight concerts outside of Europe, so again Trident and Queen lost money.

Queen had become very popular with young people in Japan, where both *Sheer Heart Attack* and "Killer Queen" were top of the charts. The Japanese **fans** wanted to see

Queen perform live, so Trident organized a tour of eight concerts in Japan. However, nobody knew if Freddie's voice would be better by the start of the Japanese tour. Queen really wanted to perform live in Japan because they had so many fans there. So Jack Nelson decided that Freddie and the band would go to Hawaii for a holiday first and then go on to Japan. When Queen finally arrived at the airport in Tokyo, they were welcomed by about 3,000 fans, all wearing Queen T-shirts. Over the next twelve days, Queen travelled around Japan, playing in concerts

Queen in Japan

on most days. The fans loved them and gave Freddie and the rest of the band lots of presents.

By now Queen were big stars, but back in London they were having serious problems with Trident about money. Freddie was not happy, because Norman Sheffield did not want to give him money to buy an expensive piano. John wanted money to buy a house, and Roger wanted money to buy a new car, but Norman did not want to give money to the band. Norman told Queen to wait until the end of the year, because all the money from Queen's records would arrive by then. But Freddie was not happy about this and could not understand why he had to wait. Queen's records were selling well, and they had won several important music prizes for best live group, best British group, best international group and best single for "Killer Queen". Freddie had also won the Ivor Novello songwriting prize for "Killer Queen".

"But we're stars," Freddie said to Norman. "We're selling millions of records."[4] Norman told Freddie again to wait until December, but Freddie became angry and argued with him. "I want it all," he shouted. "I want it now."[5] Later, in 1989, these words were in of one of Queen's songs, "I Want It All".

Queen had done very well with their hit single "Killer Queen" and their third album *Sheer Heart Attack*. But they knew that their next single had to be a big hit because they still did not have enough money. So, in August 1975, they started working on their fourth album, called

*A Night at the **Opera*** after a movie by the Marx Brothers, a family of American actors who made funny films. The four members of Queen all wrote songs for the new album. However, many months before, Freddie had begun working on a new song, "Bohemian Rhapsody", at the piano in his flat in Kensington. "Bohemian Rhapsody" lasted six minutes and was very different from other pop songs. It was in three parts, and the middle part was like opera – it was the first time that opera had been used in a pop song.

Queen were angry with Norman Sheffield because he had not wanted to give them their money. So they stopped using the Trident recording studios. They recorded the first part of "Bohemian Rhapsody" at the Rockfield Studios in Wales instead, then moved to London to finish it. It was a difficult song to record because it was very long, with many different parts for voices and guitar. Also, Freddie often wanted to change or add new things, which meant that everything had to be recorded several times. So "Bohemian Rhapsody" took about three weeks to record – the same time as a whole album would normally take. At last it was ready, and Freddie was happy with it. However, when people heard it for the first time, most of them were very surprised because they had never heard anything like it before.

Queen wanted to release "Bohemian Rhapsody" as the first single from *A Night at the Opera*, but there was a problem. The best way to promote a new song was for DJs to play it on the radio to millions of listeners. But most songs were about three minutes long, and "Bohemian Rhapsody" was nearly six minutes long, so most DJs did not want to play it. EMI, Queen's record company, asked Queen to make the song shorter, but they did not want to do that. John had written another song on the album, "You're My Best Friend". EMI asked Queen to release this as the album's first single, but the band said no.

Then Freddie's friend, the DJ Kenny Everett, heard "Bohemian Rhapsody" and loved it. When Kenny heard about their problems with getting it played on the radio, he decided to help by playing it on his show on Capital Radio. So, the next weekend, he played small parts of "Bohemian Rhapsody" to his listeners, then the whole song. He played it fourteen times over the next two days.

Hundreds of Queen fans called Capital Radio to ask about the record, and they visited record shops to try to buy it. That week, Paul Drew, an American DJ, was in London. After hearing "Bohemian Rhapsody" on the radio, he took it back to the USA, and soon many people there wanted it, too.

"Bohemian Rhapsody" was released as a single in the UK on 31st October 1975 and entered the UK charts at number forty-seven. After a week, it reached number seventeen, and then it entered the Top Ten. Queen were invited to play it on *Top of the Pops*, but they did not want to do that, because "Bohemian Rhapsody" was very difficult to play in a small TV studio. Also, Queen did not enjoy performing on *Top of the Pops*, because they could not play their songs live on the show but had to sing to a recording. So Trident made a video to go with the song, and the video was played on *Top of the Pops* instead. It was a great success, and on 25th November 1975 "Bohemian Rhapsody" became the number-one song in the UK, and it stayed at the top of the charts for the next nine weeks. *Top of the Pops* showed the video every week, and this helped to keep the song in the charts. The "Bohemian Rhapsody" video was the first music video to promote a song, and, after its success, other bands started making videos of their song, too.

A Night at the Opera reached **number one** in the UK album charts and stayed there for four weeks. For many people, it is the most famous Queen album. "Bohemian Rhapsody" is also many people's favourite Queen song. But what does the song actually mean? People have had different ideas, but nobody knows for sure. Freddie was asked many times in **interviews** what the song means, but he never gave an answer. "People still ask me what 'Bohemian Rhapsody' is all about, and I say I don't know," he said. "I think people should just listen to it, think about it, and then decide for themselves what it means to them."[6]

By the end of January 1976, "Bohemian Rhapsody" had sold more than 1 million records in the UK. It also went to number one in the singles charts in the UK,

Australia, Canada, the Netherlands, New Zealand and Belgium, and to number nine in the USA. After Freddie's death in November 1991, it went to number one in the UK again.

CHAPTER SIX
Having a good time

After the success of "Bohemian Rhapsody", Queen were on top of the world. They had millions of fans in many countries, and life would never be the same for them again. Freddie Mercury, the great rock star, was a very different person from Farrokh Bulsara, the shy young boy from Zanzibar.

But Queen's relationship with Trident had become very bad. Norman Sheffield was not happy, because Queen were always asking him for money, and Trident had lost a lot of money from Queen's tours in the USA. Queen wanted to leave Trident, and Norman agreed to this, but first they had to pay Trident £100,000.

Soon after this, Queen left Trident and got a new manager, John Reid, and a lawyer, Jim Beach. At the start of 1976, they went on another tour to the USA to promote *A Night at the Opera*. The tour started in Connecticut and then continued to New York. Freddie loved New York and had a lot of fun there. After the gigs, Queen had big parties and invited people from the world of rock and other famous guests. After the USA, they went on another tour to Japan and then Australia, and they were a great success in both countries. Queen did not have to worry about money any more, because now they were rich and famous. Freddie enjoyed spending his money and bought a lot of expensive Japanese art.

After Queen arrived back in the UK, Brian May married his girlfriend. John Deacon was also now married and had a son. One of the songs on *A Night at the Opera* was "You're My Best Friend", which John had written for his wife. It was released as a single on 18th May 1976 and reached number seven in the UK singles charts and number sixteen in the USA. So John became the second member of Queen to write a single in the UK Top Ten.

In the summer of 1976, Queen started working on their fifth album, *A Day at the Races*. Like *A Night at the Opera*, it was also named after a Marx Brothers movie. Freddie wrote four songs for the new album, including "Somebody To Love", which was released as a single on 12th November 1976. It reached number two in the UK singles charts and number thirteen in the USA. During the rest of 1976, Queen played more concerts, including a huge outdoor concert for 200,000 people in Hyde Park in London on

Queen in Hyde Park, London, September 1976

18th September. Their clothes and performance were very flamboyant, and their fans loved the show.

Freddie was still living with Mary Austin, but, by the end of 1976, she had moved out of their flat in Kensington. Some journalists started asking questions about Freddie's sexuality, and there were **rumours** that he might be gay. But Freddie did not want to answer questions about his private life. He was a great rock star with millions of fans, but he was worried that, if people knew he was bisexual, many of them would be shocked and stop buying Queen's records. So he wanted to keep his sexuality a secret, and only his best friends knew the truth. In January 1977, Queen flew back to the USA to promote *A Day at the Races*. On 5th February, they performed a show at the famous Madison Square Garden in New York, in front of an audience of 20,000 people, and it was a huge success.

Queen continued having big parties. But, although the members of the band sometimes still did things together, their lives were changing. John and Brian were spending a lot of time with their families, and Roger liked going out with members of other bands, so Freddie was often alone. He did not like this, so he often went out to gay bars and **clubs**. It was much easier for him to do this in New York than in London. Freddie felt that people in New York were not so interested in his private life, so he was free to do what he liked there, and he felt more relaxed.

In the summer of 1977, Queen wrote their sixth album, *News of the World*, and released it in October. Two of

Queen's most popular songs were on this album. The song "We Are the **Champions**" was released as a single on 7th October 1977, and it was a success all over the world. It was written by Freddie and is one of the biggest-selling singles of all time, reaching number two in the UK singles charts and number four in the US. Freddie said that, when he wrote it, he was thinking about football, and it is still often played at football games, including the 1994 FIFA World Cup. The other famous song from the *News of the World* album was "We Will Rock You", written by Brian. He wanted to write a song where the audience could sing the words, too, and make a lot of noise with their hands and feet.

At the end of 1977, Queen decided they did not need a manager any more and could manage themselves with their lawyer, Jim Beach, helping them and giving them advice. In April and May 1978, they went on tour to Europe to promote *News of the World* before coming back to the UK. Although they were very famous stars, Queen never stopped thinking about the future or writing new songs. They always worked in the same way. All the members of the band wrote songs, not just Freddie. Then they decided together which songs they liked best and recorded these for their latest album. They also decided which songs from the album to release as singles, and then they went on tour to promote the album.

By this time, Queen were very rich. However, they did not want to pay a lot of tax (money that they had to pay by law to the British government). According to the UK tax laws, they had to spend 300 days a year out of the UK in order not to pay any tax. So, in the summer of 1978, after a tour of Europe, they went to Montreux in Switzerland and to Nice in France to work on their seventh album, *Jazz*. This was the first time they had used recording studios outside the UK. Queen continued to work hard, but they enjoyed themselves, too, with huge parties for Roger's 29th birthday and Freddie's 32nd birthday in France. In July, Freddie saw the famous bicycle race the Tour de France pass through Montreux, and this gave him the idea to write the song "Bicycle Race". It was released as a single on 13th October 1978 and was a great success. Freddie also wrote "Don't Stop Me Now" for the new album. It became another best-selling single and reached number nine in the UK charts.

In the late autumn of 1978, Queen went back to the USA to promote *Jazz*, and they continued having lots of fun. By now, they were very famous in New York, both for their gigs and for their flamboyant parties after the shows. By the late 1970s, the clothes Freddie wore on stage were changing. In Queen's early days, he had worn very flamboyant clothes, but now he started wearing trousers and a cap, a popular fashion in gay nightclubs in New York at the time. In January 1979, Queen began another tour of Europe, followed by a tour of Japan. Their eighth album, *The Game*, was recorded in Musicland Studios in Munich. Freddie loved Munich and its gay bars and clubs because, like in New York, he felt very free and relaxed there.

One day, after arriving at the Hilton Hotel in Munich, Freddie decided to have a bath before going to the recording studios. Suddenly, while he was in the bath, he had an idea for a new song and asked someone to bring him a guitar. Although he was not very good at the guitar, he wrote the song in just a few minutes. He went quickly to the recording studios, where Roger and John were waiting. He told them excitedly about the new song, then played it for them. He called it "Crazy Little Thing Called Love". It was released as a single and became a huge hit all over the world. It was Queen's first number one in the USA; was top of the charts in Canada, Mexico, the Netherlands and Australia; and reached number two in the UK.

In October 1979, Freddie did something very different and exciting. He appeared in a live performance in London with the dancers of the Royal **Ballet** company while singing two of Queen's hit songs, "Bohemian Rhapsody" and "Crazy Little Thing Called Love". Everyone loved watching Freddie performing with the ballet dancers, and the show was a great success.

CHAPTER SEVEN
From rock to disco

The 1970s were really great years for Queen. They were famous rock stars with millions of fans all over the world, and they were still writing huge hits. One of the lines in a hit single that Freddie wrote, "Don't Stop Me Now", is "I'm having a good time," and it seemed that nothing could stop Queen.

By the beginning of the 1980s, Freddie was rich and famous, and he could have everything he wanted. For a long time, he had wanted to buy a house in London, but he was often away on tour or busy recording. He and Mary Austin were not lovers any more, but they were still very good friends. One day Freddie called Mary from the USA and asked her to look for a house for him. She found a wonderful house near Kensington High Street called Garden Lodge. It was very large, with eight bedrooms and a beautiful garden. When Freddie came to the UK and saw it for the first time, he loved it. He bought it immediately, although he also wanted to make some changes that would need a lot of work.

In 1980, John Deacon wrote a song for Queen's eighth album, *The Game*. At that time **disco** music was becoming very popular, so John wanted to write a song that people could dance to. The new song, "Another One Bites the Dust", was very different from Queen's other songs because it sounded more like disco than rock music. It was released on 22nd August 1980 while Queen were on tour in the USA and was a huge success. It reached number one in several different countries, including the USA, where it stayed at the top of the charts for five weeks and sold over 3 million records. This was the first time that Queen had reached number one in the US singles charts, and they were very happy, but still they wanted more. In the 2011 documentary *Queen: Days of Our Lives* (BBC), Roger Taylor said, "We didn't want just America. We wanted the whole world."[7] But perhaps Freddie knew that Queen's success could not last forever. He said in an interview in 1985, also shown on *Queen: Days of Our Lives*, "The hardest thing is to stay at the top because when you go all the way up, the only place to go after that is down."[8] But, at that moment, Queen were still at the top, and it seemed that anything was possible for them.

In the first part of 1981, they went on another tour to Japan, then did a tour of seven concerts in Argentina and Brazil. This was a very exciting chance for Queen because they had never played in South America before. Queen were so popular in Argentina and Brazil, they were asked to play in football **stadiums** there.

The concerts in South America cost a lot of money, but they were a huge success. Freddie was very good at performing in big stadiums and could easily form a relationship with thousands of fans.

Queen on tour in South America

After South America, Queen went back to Switzerland to do more recordings. By now, they had bought their own studio, Mountain Studios, in Montreux. David Bowie lived near Montreux, so they recorded a song with him, "Under Pressure", written by the band and Bowie, which reached number one in the UK singles charts.

In September, Freddie paid for a hundred of his friends to fly from London to his 35th birthday party at the Berkshire Place Hotel in New York. Then Queen went on a short tour of Venezuela and Mexico, but this tour was not a success. Some concerts were cancelled, and the band lost a lot of money, so Freddie went back to New York. Every night after dinner he went to the gay bars and clubs until the early hours of the morning and enjoyed himself.

However, at about this time people started talking about a strange and terrible new illness in the USA. Doctors did not understand exactly what this illness was, or how it was passed from one person to another, but it seemed to be especially dangerous for gay men. Many had already died, and most of those deaths had happened in New York City. The *New York Times* said that tens of thousands more gay men could be affected by the illness and not even realize for a long time that they had it. In December 1981, a UK magazine reported that a man had died in London from the same illness. The man was gay and had visited the USA many times.

After this, many gay men in the UK started to become worried about the illness. In 1982, the illness reached

Spain, France and Switzerland, and on 24th September 1982 it was given the name of AIDS (Acquired Immune Deficiency Syndrome).

At the beginning of 1982, Queen went back to Munich to record their tenth album, *Hot Space*, at the Musicland Studios. However, this album had a very different sound from Queen's other albums. Their single "Another One Bites the Dust", which sounded like disco music, had been a huge success. So Freddie thought it was a good idea for Queen's next album to sound like disco music, too. However, Roger and Brian were against this idea because they did not want Queen, which was a rock band, to change its sound to disco. They were angry with Freddie's **assistant**, Paul Prenter, because they thought he had encouraged Freddie to change Queen's sound.

Paul was a radio DJ from Belfast who had first met Freddie in a bar in 1975 and became his assistant in 1977. Freddie often listened to Paul and followed his advice. The other members of the band did not like Paul very much and did not think he was a very good friend to Freddie. He encouraged Freddie to go to parties, and he never told Freddie to be more careful about his life. "[Paul] was a very, very bad influence on Freddie," said Roger. "He very much wanted our music to sound like music in a gay club. And I didn't."[9]

A few months later in 1982, the band went on tour in the UK and Europe to promote *Hot Space*. However, this tour was not a success, because many of Queen's fans were surprised by the disco sound of the new album, and they did not like it. Although *Hot Space* reached number four in the UK album charts, it only reached number twenty-two in the USA.

By now, Freddie had changed a lot and looked very different from the glam-rock singer of the 1970s. He had very short hair and a black moustache, and he often appeared on stage wearing a T-shirt, a cap and jeans.

Later in 1982, Queen went on tour to Canada, the USA and Japan to promote *Hot Space*. They still had many fans in Japan, so the tour there went well, but in the USA they were not as popular as they had been before. At the end of 1981, Queen had been one of the most famous bands in the world, but now, less than a year later, other bands and singers were doing better than Queen. *Hot Space* sold about 4 million records in the world, but Michael Jackson's new album, *Thriller*, sold over 65 million.

Queen were also having problems because they were not happy with Elektra, their record company in the USA. They did not think Elektra had promoted *Hot Space* very well, so Freddie decided he would not work with them any more. Also, after the tour in Japan, Freddie and the other members of Queen did not have the same good relationship as before, because of what had happened with *Hot Space* and Paul Prenter's influence over Freddie.

Freddie with short hair and a moustache in 1982

Freddie had often thought about making an album by himself, and he decided that now was the right time. So Queen's lawyer and manager, Jim Beach, organized a deal for Freddie with the US record company Capital Records. But the other members of Queen were not happy about this deal, because Capital paid Freddie more money for his album than other albums that Queen had made.

CHAPTER EIGHT
The end of Queen?

Freddie went back to the recording studios in Munich to start work on his album, *Mr Bad Guy*. During the next few months, he did not see much of the other members of Queen. Paul Prenter was staying with him in Munich, and, after Freddie had finished work at the studios, Freddie and Paul spent a lot of time together in the gay bars and clubs. Freddie made lots of new friends, too. He continued going to parties and having a good time. He did not seem worried about AIDS and was not very careful about his life. The DJ Paul Gambaccini, an old friend of Freddie's, met Freddie in a club in New York in 1983. Paul talked about the new illness, but Freddie just waved his arms and did not seem to care.

Freddie and the other members of Queen came together again in August 1983 to record their eleventh album, *The Works*, in California. This was released in the UK by EMI Records in February 1984 and reached number two in the UK album charts. In the USA, it was the band's first album that was released by their new record company, Capital Records. The first single to be released from the album was "Radio Ga Ga", which was written by Roger Taylor. It quickly became a huge hit, reaching number two in the UK singles charts and number sixteen in the USA. Audiences all over the world loved the song because they could sing the words, too, and clap their hands. Now each of the four members of Queen had written a hit song that had reached the UK Top Ten singles charts. They were the only band in the world to achieve this. In April 1984, Queen released a second single from *The Works* called "I Want to Break Free", which was written by John Deacon. It reached number three in the UK charts, did well in other countries in Europe and was very popular with fans across most of the world.

However, "I Want to Break Free" was not a success in the USA, one of the most important countries for Queen. It did not sell well there because of the video that Queen made to promote it. This video was very different from their other videos. It showed the four members of the band dressed like women on *Coronation Street*, a popular British TV show. At the start of the video, Freddie appeared as a housewife cleaning the house. He was wearing a wig, which was made of black hair, and lots of make-up. He also wore

Freddie dressed up as a housewife

a short, black skirt and a pink blouse. Roger was dressed like a schoolgirl, while Brian and John were dressed like old ladies reading newspapers. Many people in Britain thought this video was very funny, especially as Freddie still had his big, black moustache. However, people in the USA did not like it, and one of the top TV stations in the USA said they would not play it. So, when Queen went on tour to promote the album in 1984 and 1985, they did not go to the USA, because it seemed that their success there was ending.

Queen in "I Want to Break Free"

There were problems with the song in other countries, too. In the video, the four "women" want to escape or "break free" from their boring lives by dreaming of exciting new lives as famous rock stars. Queen had only meant this in a fun way. But in some places, like South America, people who had not seen the video thought the song carried a serious message against the government. So when Queen played the song on tour in Rio de Janeiro in January 1985, and Freddie came on stage dressed in women's clothes and a wig, the audience did not like it. They were very angry because, for them, it was a serious song. So they started shouting and throwing stones and shoes at Freddie. But when he took off his wig and women's clothes, they stopped throwing things and became quiet.

In 1984, Queen had had another bad experience. They went to South Africa because they were paid a lot of money to play in some concerts in Sun City in Bophuthatswana. But many of Queen's fans were angry with them for going to South Africa and said that Queen had made a terrible mistake. This was because, at that time, there was still **apartheid** in South Africa, and people thought that, by performing there, Queen were supporting apartheid. So, at the start of 1985, things were not going well for Queen. They were not at the top of the UK charts any more, and people had stopped buying their records in the USA. They had made many of their fans in South America and other places angry. Also, the four members of the band were not spending much time together any more.

Freddie had released his own single, "Love Kills", which had reached number ten in the UK, higher than Queen's last single, "Hammer to Fall". Their private lives had become more separate, too. Brian, Roger and John all had families and were spending a lot of time with them, but Freddie's life was very different. He was living in Munich, having fun and going to parties and clubs with Paul Prenter and his other friends. Many fans were beginning to ask what was happening to the band. "Is this the end of Queen?" they asked, sadly.

But something was happening in Africa that would change everything for Queen. Between 1983 and 1985, there was a terrible **famine** in Ethiopia, and about 1 million people died because they did not have enough to eat. Bob Geldof, a famous Irish singer and songwriter, saw reports about the famine on TV. So, in 1984, he travelled to Ethiopia himself and was very shocked. He decided he had to do something to help the people of Ethiopia. So, after he returned to the UK, Bob and another singer, Midge Ure, formed a huge pop group called Band Aid. They invited a lot of famous British and Irish singers and musicians to join the new group.

On 3rd December 1984, Band Aid released a single called "Do They Know It's Christmas?" Bob wrote the words, and Midge wrote the music. It was very difficult to organize because there were so many different bands and singers, but the recording was done in just one day,

THE END OF QUEEN?

Bono, Paul McCartney and Freddie singing together

on 25th November. It quickly became Britain's fastest and best-selling single ever, selling over 3 million records in the UK before the end of the year and making £8 million to help the people of Ethiopia. After Band Aid, another large group was formed in the USA called USA for Africa. They released the single "We Are the World", which sold 20 million records and made $63 million.

CHAPTER NINE

"We Are the Champions"

Bob Geldof was very happy with the success of "Do They Know It's Christmas?", but now he began to think about what more he could do for the people of Ethiopia. Then he had a very exciting idea – to organize a huge outdoor concert called Live Aid and give all the money that people paid for tickets to help Ethiopia. So, during the first few months of 1985, he contacted many of the top bands and singers in the UK and Ireland and asked them to play for free in the Live Aid concert. Queen were on tour in New Zealand, but Bob contacted their lawyer and manager, Jim Beach. He spoke to Freddie and the other band members, and they agreed to perform.

Queen wanted to help the people of Ethiopia, but they also knew that Live Aid was very important for them as a band. They were not at the top of the charts any more, and they had lost a lot of fans because many people were not happy about their concerts in South Africa. Also, there were many talented new bands and singers who were younger than Queen and who were becoming very popular. Queen knew that, at the Live Aid concert, the eyes of the world would be on them, and they wanted to do their best. They decided not to promote their new songs in the concert but to play songs that the audience knew and loved. So they carefully planned which songs they were going to sing and chose six of their most famous hits. However, each band was only allowed twenty minutes to perform, so Queen had to make some of their songs shorter. They worked very hard for three days, rehearsing their songs.

Bob Geldof organized Live Aid in only ten weeks. It happened on 13th July 1985, continued for sixteen hours and was held in two countries at the same time – the UK and the USA. In the UK the bands played at Wembley Football Stadium in London, and in the USA they played at the John F. Kennedy Stadium in Philadelphia. The audience at Wembley was about 70,000 people, and in Philadelphia it was about 100,000 people. The two concerts were joined by **satellite** TV, so people all over the world could watch the bands and singers performing live in both countries. After each band in the UK had finished playing, the stage was made ready for the next band. While this was happening, the audience in the UK could watch a band in the USA. At the same time, smaller concerts were held in other countries, including the Soviet Union, Canada, Japan, Germany, Australia, Austria, Holland and Yugoslavia. These concerts were also joined to the Live Aid concert by satellite TV.

The weather on the day of the show in the UK was warm and sunny. The concert began at noon, with the first rock band, Status Quo, singing their hit

"Rockin' All Over the World". They were followed by many other famous bands. The audience were having a wonderful time in the afternoon sun, watching the bands and listening to the great music. Band followed band, until it was time for Queen to perform. But now there was a problem with Freddie's voice. A doctor was called, and the doctor told Freddie he was too ill to sing. But Freddie did not want to listen to the doctor's advice, because nothing was going to stop him from performing.

Millions of people were waiting to hear Queen, not only in the audience at Wembley but also all over the world. So, at 6.44 p.m., Freddie and the other members of Queen ran on to the stage. Freddie was wearing jeans and a white top and looked very healthy. Nobody guessed that

Queen at Live Aid

Freddie on stage

there was anything wrong with him. As Queen got ready to play, the audience cheered loudly. When the band looked across the stadium, they saw thousands of happy and excited faces welcoming them.

Freddie sat down at the piano and immediately began to play "Bohemian Rhapsody". As soon as the audience heard this famous song, they cheered again and waved their arms from side to side. After some minutes, Queen continued with another of their big hits, "Radio Ga Ga". Freddie jumped up from the piano and danced across the stage, while the audience sang with him and clapped their hands. Queen's third

Queen at Live Aid

song was "Hammer to Fall", and, again, Freddie danced around the stage. Next, he took a guitar and started playing and singing "Crazy Little Thing Called Love".

The audience were having a really good time, clapping and singing. Finally, Queen played two more of their famous hits – "We Will Rock You" and "We Are the Champions". Both of these songs were especially popular with live audiences.

As Freddie sat down at the piano and sang "We Are the Champions", thousands of people across the stadium sang with him and waved their arms. It was very important to Freddie to make his audience feel happy. His live performances were always amazing because he could form a great relationship with his audience, and he knew how to control them. But this was the greatest performance of his life.

Bob Geldof had hoped that the Live Aid concert would make £10 million in the UK, but it made more than £30 million. There were eight places across the UK where people could call to give money. Many famous bands and singers played at Live Aid that day, and there were some great performances, but, for many people, Queen were the stars of the show. Later, Bob Geldof said in an interview, "Queen were the best band of the day. They played the best, had the best sound . . . They understood the idea of Live Aid exactly . . . They played one hit after another . . . It was the best stage for Freddie: the whole world."[10] On that day, Queen really were the champions of the world, and some people think their performance at Live Aid was the greatest rock performance ever.

Freddie had invited a new friend, Jim Hutton, to the Live Aid concert. Freddie had first seen Jim in late 1983 in a gay club in South Kensington, and Freddie had liked him very much. He had wanted to buy Jim a drink, but Jim was with his boyfriend, so he said no. Later, his boyfriend told him the man was the famous rock star Freddie Mercury. But, at that time, Jim did not know who Freddie Mercury was, and he had never heard of Queen. Although he liked listening to pop music on the radio at work, he did not know the names of the bands who played it. Four or five months later, Jim and his boyfriend were having dinner in a restaurant in West London. Suddenly his boyfriend said, "Oh, your friend is here."[11] Jim turned round and saw Freddie, but Freddie did not see him.

The next time that Jim and Freddie met was the night of Saturday 23rd March 1984, at a club called Heaven near Charing Cross Station. Freddie was at the club with a crowd of friends. When he saw Jim, he again wanted to buy him a drink, and, this time, Jim agreed. Freddie invited Jim to join his friends, and everybody had fun, dancing till about four in the morning. Then they went back to Freddie's flat to continue the party. The next day, after everybody had left, Jim and Freddie talked.

Jim told Freddie that he was a hairdresser, and Freddie just said, "I'm a singer."[12] After that, Jim did not see Freddie again for three months, and then Freddie called Jim and invited him to his flat for dinner. Freddie explained that he had not contacted Jim because he had been in Munich, where he lived most of the time. He had also been on a tour of Australia, New Zealand and Japan with his band, Queen.

The next Friday, when Jim was at work, someone from the Queen office called him to say that Freddie was inviting him to Munich for the weekend. Jim was not rich, so he could not afford a plane ticket to Munich, but the man told him that Freddie would pay for everything. When Jim arrived in Munich, Freddie was waiting excitedly at the airport with some friends. Jim had a wonderful weekend, staying with Freddie in his flat and going out to the clubs with Freddie and his friends. During the next months, Jim went to Germany several times to see Freddie, and, each time, they became more important to each other.

Although Freddie was still living in Munich, he was beginning to spend more time in London. Soon Freddie introduced Jim to another important person in his life, Mary Austin. One Sunday after breakfast, Freddie invited Jim and Mary and several other friends to his flat in Kensington. "We're going for a walk,"[13] he told them. It was a beautiful sunny morning, and, after about twenty minutes, they came to a gate in a long, high wall. Freddie opened the gate, and they entered a large and wonderful garden. It was the garden of Garden Lodge, the beautiful old house that Freddie had bought at the end of the 1970s. Freddie had wanted to make several changes to the house, which had cost a lot of money and taken a long time to finish. But now the builders had gone, and it was almost ready for Freddie to move into. Jim was very surprised by the beautiful house, and he especially loved the garden.

Although Jim had known Freddie for several months, he had never seen him perform. On the day of the Live Aid concert, Saturday 13th July, Jim went round to Freddie's flat after work. Freddie and lots of his friends were there, watching the concert on TV, and Jim sat down to join them. He was still wearing his work clothes. At about four in the afternoon, Freddie turned to Jim and said, "Aren't you going to get ready? We're going to Live Aid!"[14]

Freddie gave Jim some jeans and a top to wear instead of his work clothes. Soon they were sitting in the back of a huge, black car on their way to Wembley. When they arrived, Jim was very surprised because there were famous rock stars everywhere. When it was time

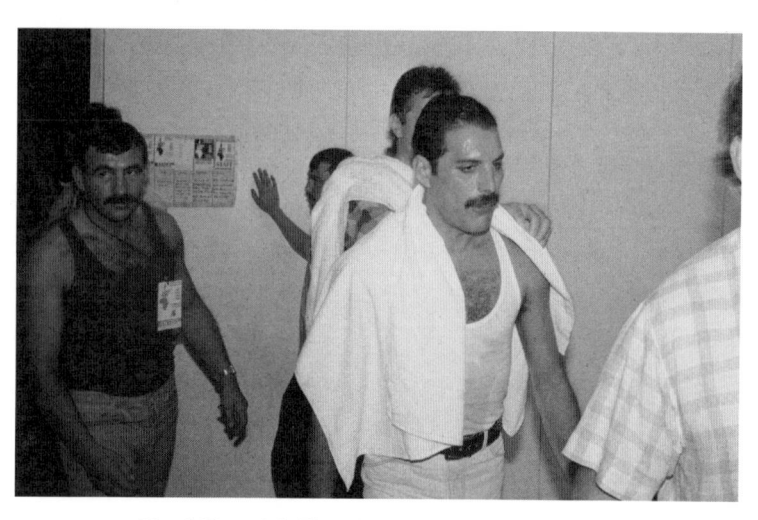

Freddie with Jim, backstage at Live Aid

for Queen to perform, Jim walked with Freddie to the stage and stood at the side while Queen played six of their most famous hits in front of a live audience of 70,000 people. As the audience sang happily and waved their arms, Jim realized that Freddie really was a great rock star, loved by millions of fans everywhere.

CHAPTER TEN
The last years

After the Live Aid concert, Queen were back on top. They had shown everyone that they were still one of the greatest rock bands in the world. During the next few years, they recorded more songs together and had several big hits. In March 1986, they released a single, "A Kind of Magic", that reached number three in the UK charts. The album of the same name was released in June 1986 and reached number one in the UK album charts. Several of the songs from the album were used as music for the movie *Highlander*. Queen went on tour in Europe to promote the album, returning to the UK in July. That month they played two concerts at Wembley Stadium, where every ticket was sold.

By the end of 1985, Freddie was becoming tired of the parties and clubs in Munich. So he decided to go back to Garden Lodge, and soon Jim Hutton came to live with him there. Freddie was living with somebody he loved, and he was very happy, but now there were more rumours in the media about Freddie's sexuality. Freddie did not want journalists to know that he was gay, or to write about his relationship with Jim. In July 1986, after one of the concerts at Wembley, Queen gave a big party, and a lot of people from the media were there, taking photographs. So Freddie went to the party with Mary Austin because he wanted them to think that she was still his girlfriend. At the end of September 1986, Freddie and Jim went to Japan for a holiday. But, when they returned to London three weeks later, a journalist was waiting for Freddie at Heathrow Airport. He asked Freddie about a story in the *News of the World* newspaper with the title "Queen Star Freddie in AIDS shock". "Is it true you have AIDS?" asked the journalist. "Do I look like I'm dying?" replied Freddie, angrily. "Go away and leave me alone."[15]

In January 1987, Freddie recorded a number of songs by himself, including "The Great Pretender". This became the biggest hit he made alone, and it reached number four in the UK singles charts. A video was made to promote the song, and Freddie wore a flamboyant pink suit in it. Freddie liked the song because it was about himself. "Most of the things I do are pretending," he said. "It's like acting. I go on stage and pretend . . . I think 'The Great Pretender' is a great title for what I do because I *am* The Great Pretender!"[16] Freddie was still doing exciting new things. He liked the voice of the famous Spanish opera singer Montserrat Caballé. In the spring of 1987, he met Montserrat in Barcelona and was very pleased when she asked him to write some music for her.

But in April 1987, Freddie had some very bad news. He was tested for AIDS, and the results showed that he

**Freddie with the Spanish opera singer
Montserrat Caballé**

had this terrible illness. He went to other doctors, but the results were the same. At that time, a person with AIDS could not expect to live longer than about three years. Several of Freddie's friends with AIDS had already died, so Freddie knew there was very little hope for him. He told a few good friends, like Mary Austin and Jim Beach, that he had AIDS. Jim Hutton was in Ireland visiting his mother, and, the next day, when Jim got back to Garden Lodge, Freddie told him about the test results. "If you want to leave me and move out of Garden Lodge, I won't stop you; I'll understand," he said to Jim. Jim was very sad and shocked, but he did not want to leave Freddie. "But I love you," he said. "I'm not going to walk away from you – now or ever. Let's not talk about it any more."[17]

Then another terrible thing happened. In 1986, Paul Prenter, Freddie's assistant, had had nowhere to live, so Freddie had lent Paul the keys to his flat in London. But Paul had had a party in the flat without telling Freddie, and his friends had done a lot of damage. Freddie was very angry with Paul and told him to leave his job. Because of this, Paul wanted to hurt Freddie. So he sold information about Freddie's private life to the *Sun* newspaper for £32,000, together with photographs of Freddie's lovers. On 4th May 1987, a story appeared in the *Sun* with the title "AIDS Kills Freddie's Two Lovers". It said that Freddie had slept with a lot of men, and two of them had died. Paul also told the *Sun* about Freddie's relationship with Jim Hutton.

Many people in Britain were very shocked by the story, and Freddie was very angry. He spent as much time as possible behind the high walls of Garden Lodge with Jim, who was now working as Freddie's gardener. Sometimes he had to go out to visit doctors, but there were always people from the media outside waiting for him. So he decided to escape from London and go to Ibiza with Jim and two other friends. While he was there, he and

Montserrat Caballé sang together in a show before an audience of 6,000 people. The song was called "Barcelona" and was a huge success. Later it was chosen to be the song for the **Olympics** in Barcelona. After Ibiza, Freddie and Jim went back to Garden Lodge and lived there quietly for the rest of the year. They did not go out much, but they sometimes invited friends for small dinner parties, played games, sang songs or watched TV.

In early 1988, Queen started work on a new album, *The Miracle*, and they recorded twenty-two songs. For the first time, they said these songs were written by the band "Queen" and not by different members of the band. They continued working on *The Miracle* later in the year, and Freddie also recorded songs with Montserrat Caballé for their *Barcelona* album. On 14th April 1988, he appeared live for the last time at a performance at London's Dominion Theatre and sang four songs. But, by now, there were more rumours in the media that Freddie could have AIDS. The other members of Queen knew that he was not well, but they did not know what was wrong with him. At the end of 1988, Freddie went back to Munich with Jim and two friends, but he felt too ill to visit the bars and clubs. In a radio interview in March 1989, Freddie said he did not want to go on tour to promote *The Miracle*. Rumours immediately started that Freddie was ill, but the other band members always told everyone that he was very healthy. But Freddie knew he had to tell the band the truth, so, in May 1989, he finally told them he had AIDS.

Brian, Roger and John were very shocked and sad, but they wanted to help Freddie as much as possible. When people asked how he was, they said he was fine. *The Miracle* was released on 22nd May 1989 and reached number one in the UK album charts. Freddie was still not ready to stop making music. He wanted to get back into the studios and record as many new songs as possible before he died. So Freddie and Queen went back to Mountain Studios in Montreux to record another album. Freddie loved the clean mountain air of Montreux. In London there were always journalists waiting for him outside Garden Lodge, but in Montreux nobody was interested in his private life, and he could do what he liked there.

By now, many people were asking questions about Freddie, but the other members of Queen continued to say that there was nothing wrong with him. Back in London, he stayed at home at Garden Lodge as much as possible, with only a few good friends around him. In August 1990, he told his sister Kashmira and her husband that he had AIDS, but not his parents. In September 1990, he had a dinner party for his 44th birthday at Garden Lodge for his dearest friends. But Freddie was getting thinner and looking more ill all the time. One day, the *Sun* published a photo of Freddie outside a doctor's with the title "The Sad Face of

Freddie Mercury". People in Britain were very shocked by this picture because Freddie looked like an old man.

On 26th January 1991, Queen were at the top of the UK singles charts again with the hit single from their new album, *Innuendo*. The album, which was released in February, reached number one in the UK, the Netherlands, Germany, Italy and Switzerland. Late in the spring, Freddie and Queen were still recording in the Montreux studios. The three other members of Queen were living in Montreux, ready to come to the studios when Freddie felt well enough, but they knew that they did not have much more time. Freddie could only walk very slowly, and for much of the time he was in great pain. In May 1991, he came back to London to make a video to promote the song "These Are the Days of Our Lives", written by Roger Taylor. By now, Freddie was very weak, so it was decided to make the video in black and white to try to hide his illness. He had to stand in the same place for most of the time because it hurt him to move. In the video, which was Freddie's last, he gave a wonderful performance. At the end, he looked into the camera, smiled and said, "I still love you." For many of his fans, this was his way of saying goodbye.

Later in 1991, Freddie went back to Montreux but finally returned to Garden Lodge on Sunday 10th November. The journalists were still waiting outside, asking anybody who was going in or out of the house for news of Freddie. Sometimes they even climbed on to the

One of the last photos of Freddie, taken about six months before he died

walls and looked down into the garden. During the week of Monday 18th November, Freddie's family came to visit him. On 21st November, he was seen for the last time at his bedroom window, calling down to Jim in the garden. On Friday 22nd November, Freddie sent a message to Jim Beach, Queen's lawyer and manager, asking him to come and see him. He had decided to tell the world that he had AIDS.

At midnight, Jim went outside and read this information from Freddie to the journalists. It said: "I wish to [say] that I . . . have AIDS . . . the time has come now for my friends and fans around the world to know the truth and I hope that everyone will join with my doctors . . . in the fight against this terrible illness."[18] On the evening of Sunday 24th November 1991, Freddie died.

Garden Lodge

After Freddie's death, Queen released a single of "Bohemian Rhapsody" and "These Are the Days of Our Lives". It went

Concert at Wembley Stadium to remember Freddie

immediately to the top of the UK charts and stayed there for five weeks. During this time, Queen also had ten albums in the UK album charts. People all over the world had read about Freddie's death in the newspapers. Hundreds of people had died of AIDS before Freddie, but very few were as famous as he was. So now more people began to learn about AIDS and understand this terrible illness better.

THE LAST YEARS

On 20th April 1992, Brian, Roger and John organized a concert to remember Freddie at Wembley Stadium. Many of the biggest stars in the world came to sing Queen's greatest hits in front of an audience of 72,000 people. The concert was broadcast to seventy-six countries around the world and made £12 million for the fight against AIDS. Brian, Roger and John were happy that the concert was a success, but they were also very sad because Freddie would never sing with them again.

But Freddie's death was not the end of Queen. On 6th November 1995, Queen released a new album, *Made in Heaven*, with thirteen songs. Freddie had recorded some of these songs with Queen during his last weeks, and two were songs he had recorded alone. The album went to number one in the UK album charts and sold over 10 million records.

Over the next few years, Queen released albums of their greatest hits. In 2002, *We Will Rock You*, a theatre show about Queen's music, opened in London and ran for twelve years.

John left Queen, but Brian and Roger did not want people to forget the band. They started going on world tours with different singers taking Freddie's place. In 2009, Brian saw a young American, Adam Lambert, singing "Bohemian Rhapsody" on an American TV show. He liked Adam's voice very much, and, after that, Adam often went on tour with Brian and Roger.

Queen's music is still loved by people all over the world. In October 2018, a film, *Bohemian Rhapsody*, was released, with the actor Rami Malek playing the part of Freddie. It tells the story of Freddie and Queen from the start of the rock band to their famous performance at the Live Aid concert in 1985. The movie was a huge success, and, in 2019, Rami won the Oscar for Best Actor. *Bohemian Rhapsody* helped people understand more not only about Freddie's music but also about his private life and relationships. He was an amazingly talented musician and a great rock star, who people will love and remember for many years.

During-reading questions

Write the answers to these questions in your notebook.

CHAPTER ONE

1. Who were the members of Freddie's family?
2. Where did Freddie go to school?
3. Why did the Bulsara family leave Zanzibar?
4. How was life for the Bulsaras when they first arrived in London?

CHAPTER TWO

1. Why was London very exciting for Freddie?
2. How was Freddie's dream about his future different from his parents' dream for him?
3. What lucky chance did Freddie get in the spring of 1970?

CHAPTER THREE

1. Why was Biba a very popular shop in the 1960s?
2. How did Freddie meet Mary Austin?
3. How did Mary feel after Freddie told her that he was bisexual?

CHAPTER FOUR

1. What deal did the Sheffield brothers make with Queen?
2. How was *Sounds of the Seventies* important for Queen?
3. Why didn't things go well for Queen in Australia?
4. What exciting chance did Queen have in February 1974?

CHAPTER FIVE

1. Why were Queen not happy with Trident in 1975? What did Trident tell the band to do?
2. How was "Bohemian Rhapsody" different from other pop songs?
3. How did Queen get "Bohemian Rhapsody" played on the radio?
4. Why did Queen make a video to go with "Bohemian Rhapsody"? What was special about this?

CHAPTER SIX

1. Who was the second member of Queen to write a Top-Ten single?
2. Why did Freddie have to keep his sexuality a secret?
3. Where did Freddie write "Crazy Little Thing Called Love"?

CHAPTER SEVEN

1. What was Queen's first number-one single in the USA?
2. How was that single different from Queen's other songs?
3. Why was Roger Taylor not happy with Paul?

CHAPTER EIGHT

1. Why were many of Queen's fans angry with them?
2. What problems did Queen have at the start of 1985?
3. Why did many people in Ethiopia die between 1983 and 1985?

CHAPTER NINE

1. What happened at the Live Aid concert?
2. What did Queen do to make their performance at Live Aid a success?
3. How did Freddie first meet Jim Hutton?
4. Why was Jim surprised at the Live Aid concert?

CHAPTER TEN

1. Why did Freddie go to the party in 1986 with Mary and not Jim?
2. What terrible news did Freddie get in 1987?
3. Why and how did Paul Prenter hurt Freddie?
4. Why did Freddie ask Jim Beach to come and see him?

After-reading questions

1 Look at "Before-reading question 2". Do you know all of the answers to the questions now?

2 How did Freddie change in the book?

3 Who are these people? Why were they important in Freddie's life?
   a Brian May
   b Mary Austin
   c Paul Prenter
   d Jim Hutton

4 How were the members of Queen (a) similar (b) different?

5 Freddie said, "*I am* the Great Pretender." Why did he say this? What things did Freddie pretend about in his life?

6 What mistakes, if any, did Freddie and Queen make, do you think?

7 Do you agree that Freddie was a great rock star? Give your reasons.

Exercises

CHAPTER ONE

1 Are these sentences *true* or *false*? Write the correct answers in your notebook.
1. Freddie Mercury's birthday was 5th September. ...*true*...
2. Bomi and Jer Bulsara first met in Zanzibar.
3. Freddie's parents sent him to school in London.
4. In his first band, The Hectics, Freddie was the lead singer.
5. At first, life in London was difficult for the Bulsaras.
6. Brian May and his dad built a guitar together.

CHAPTER TWO

2 In your notebook, make words from the letters.
1. Many teenagers in the 1960s had **stirrnasot** radios.
   ...*transistor*...
2. *Top of the Pops* was a popular TV **wsoh**.
3. Bands wanted to appear on TV to **ootrmep** their new songs.
4. Radio Caroline was the name of a **eitarp** radio.
5. Freddie's parents wanted him to be a **wylare**.
6. Freddie wrote songs and hid them under his **lwiopl**.
7. Tim and Brian advertised for a **emrumrd**.

CHAPTER THREE

3 Make these sentences reported speech in your notebook.
1. Freddie said to Brian, "I like Mary."
   Freddie told Brian that he liked Mary.
2. Brian said to Freddie, "Mary is just a friend."
3. Freddie said to Roger, "I'm waiting to see Mary."
4. Mary said to her friend, "Freddie is not happy."
5. Freddie said to Mary, "I'm bisexual."
6. Then he said to her, "I will always love you."

CHAPTER FOUR

4 Complete these sentences in your notebook, using the names from the box.

| The Sheffield brothers   EMI   Jack Nelson   Freddie Mercury |
| Kenny Everett   "Killer Queen"   David Bowie |

1 *The Sheffield brothers* owned Trident Studios.
2 .... was Queen's first manager.
3 .... was a top record company in London.
4 .... wrote most of Queen's songs.
5 .... was Queen's biggest hit single in 1974.
6 .... invited Freddie to be a guest on his radio show.
7 .... cancelled a show on *Top of the Pops*.

CHAPTER FIVE

5 Complete these sentences in your notebook, using the words from the box.

| cancel   opera   organized   album   released |
| international   hit   fans |

1 Freddie did not want to *cancel* the concert in Washington and make his audience sad.
2 Trident .... eight concerts for Queen in Japan.
3 Thousands of Japanese .... were waiting for Queen at Tokyo Airport.
4 Queen won several big prizes, including best .... group.
5 *Sheer Heart Attack* was the name of Queen's third ....
6 They knew that "Bohemian Rhapsody" had to be a big ....
7 The middle part of the song was like ....
8 "Bohemian Rhapsody" was .... as a single on 31st October 1975.

CHAPTER SIX

6 **Complete these sentences with the correct form of the verb in your notebook.**

1 By the start of 1976, Queen's relationship with Trident **became / *had become*** very bad.
2 At that time Norman was not happy with Queen, because he **lost / had lost** a lot of money.
3 A new hit single **was released / has been released** by Queen on 18th May 1976.
4 By the end of 1976, Mary **had moved / moved** out of the flat in Kensington.
5 If people knew Freddie was gay, perhaps they **will stop / would stop** buying Queen's records.
6 Queen left the UK because they **had not wanted / did not want** to pay a lot of tax.

CHAPTER EIGHT

7 **Complete these sentences with the correct word in your notebook.**

The years 1984 and 1985 were not good for Queen. At a [1] **recording / *concert*** in Rio de Janeiro, Freddie was wearing a short black skirt and a black [2] **hair / wig**. The people in the [3] **audience / clubs** threw stones and shoes at him. Queen had also been to South Africa. But a lot of their [4] **fans / audience** were not happy about this, because they thought Queen was supporting [5] **famine / apartheid**. Between 1983 and 1985, there was a terrible [6] **famine / apartheid** in Ethiopia. The Irish singer and songwriter Bob Geldof [7] **formed / made** a huge pop group, and on 25th November they [8] **recorded / promoted** a song called "Do They Know It's Christmas?".

CHAPTER NINE

8 Put the sentences in the correct order in your notebook.

a ...*1*... Bob Geldof invited Queen to play at the Live Aid concert.
b .... Jim and Freddie went to the concert in a large black car.
c .... Jim went to Freddie's flat to watch Live Aid on TV.
d .... Queen rehearsed six of their greatest hits for three days.
e .... Queen played at Live Aid.
f .... Freddie gave Jim some jeans and a top.

CHAPTER TEN

9 Who is thinking this, do you think? Write the correct name in your notebook.

| Jim | Freddie | Paul | Brian | Kashmira | Mary |

1 "I love Freddie. I know he's ill, but I will never leave him." ...*Jim*..
2 "Why don't the journalists go away and stop asking me stupid questions?"
3 "I don't want people to forget Queen. Maybe we can find another singer to come on tour."
4 "Freddie hurt me. Now I want to hurt him as much as I can."
5 "I don't want mum and dad to find out that Freddie has AIDS."
6 "I remember when Freddie used to come into Biba. He was so shy."

Project work

1 Look online, and find out about the 1985 Live Aid concert. Choose another band (or singer) in the concert, either in London or Philadelphia, and find out:
   a how many people were in the band
   b what kind of music they played
   c what they looked like
   d their most famous song(s)
   e how they started and how they then became famous.
   Tell your friends about them.

2 It is a year after Freddie's death. Imagine you are a journalist doing an interview with one or more of these people. Write down some questions you plan to ask them, and write what their answers might be.
   a Jer Bulsara
   b the other members of Queen
   c Mary Austin
   d Jim Hutton

3 Choose your favourite Queen song, and find out more about it. Think about:
   a who wrote it and when
   b what it is about
   c why you like it.
   Make a presentation to share with your friends.

An answer key for all questions and exercises can be found at **www.penguinreaders.co.uk**

Glossary

album (n.)
a group of songs or pieces of music on a CD, record, computer, etc. *Musicians* make and sell *albums*.

apartheid (n.)
in the past in South Africa, when white people made things very difficult for black people, and black people had to live in separate places to white people

assistant (n.)
someone whose job is to help another person with their work

audience (n.)
all the people who are watching a play, film or *concert*

ballet (n.)
a type of dancing that tells a story with music and no words

bass (adj.)
a deep sound in music. A *bass* guitar has a deep, repeated sound.

bisexual (adj.)
A person who is *bisexual* has sex with both men and women.

broadcast (v.)
to send out sounds and pictures on TV or radio

cancel (v.)
to say that something you have planned for the future will not happen

champion (n.)
a person who wins a competition

charts (n.)
a list (= a set of words that are written one below the other) that shows the best-selling songs of each week

club (n.)
a place where people dance and drink at night

concert (n.)
when people play music or sing in a place and a lot of other people listen to them

date (n.)
when two people who are in a *relationship* meet and go out somewhere together

deal (n.)
A *deal* is when you agree to work, or to buy or sell something, at a price.

designer (n.)
A fashion *designer* is a person whose job is to plan how clothes will look.

disc jockey (n.)
someone who plays music on the radio or in a *club*

disco (adj.)
A *disco* is a place where people dance to *popular* music, or "*disco*" music.

drummer (n.)
a person who plays the drums
(= a thing that you use to play music. You hit it with long pieces of wood called sticks.)

equipment (n.)
all the machines and other things that you need to do a job

especially (adv.)
more than normal

exactly (adv.)
You use "*exactly*" when you are giving information that is correct in every way.

famine (n.)
when there is not enough food in a country, and many people become ill or die

fan (n.)
someone who likes a famous person, sport, or type of music very much

flamboyant (adj.)
wearing interesting clothes or doing different things that make other people notice you

form (v.)
You *form* something by putting several people or parts together.

gay (adj.)
A *gay* man has sex with other men. A *gay* woman has sex with other women.

gig (n.)
when a singer or band plays music in front of an *audience*

government (n.)
a group of important people who decide what must happen in a country

hit (adj. and n.)
a song or piece of music that a lot of people buy

including (prep.)
when something or someone is part of a larger group or amount

influence (n.)
something that can change what a person thinks or does. It is a good or bad *influence* on them.

international (adj.)
for or by two or more countries

interview (n.)
when someone asks you questions to learn information about you

lawyer (n.)
A *lawyer* helps people with the law.

lead (adj.)
A *lead* singer in a band is the person who sings the most.

live (adj.)
A *live performance* is seen or heard by people at the same time as it happens. It is not recorded.

make-up (n.)
special colours that you put on your face to make you look different or more beautiful

member (n.)
someone who belongs to a group

musician (n.)
someone who plays music or sings, often as a job

number-one (adj.); **number one** (n.)
A song or *album* is *number one* if it is at the top of the *charts*.

Olympics (n.)
a famous *international* sports competition that happens every four years

opera (n.)
a type of play when the actors sing most of the words

organize (v.)
to plan something and make it happen

perform (v.); **performance** (n.)
To *perform* is to sing, act or play music in front of an *audience*. A *performance* is when singers, actors or *musicians* do this.

pillow (n.)
a soft thing that you put your head on when you are in bed

popular (adj.)
liked by a lot of people

pretend (v.)
to make people think that something is true when it is not

prize (n.)
money or a nice thing that you give to someone who wins a competition

promote (v.)
to advertise something

record (n.)
A *record* plays music with a special machine. It is made from plastic and is flat, round and black.

rehearse (v.)
to practise music, dance or a play before a *performance*

relationship (n.)
A *relationship* is a special friendship where two people love each other and have sex; it is also the way people are when they are together. If they like each other, they have a good *relationship*. If they do not like each other, they have a bad *relationship*.

release (v.)
to make it possible for people to hear and buy an *album* or song

revolution (n.)
when people change the *government* of their country by fighting against it

rock (adj.)
Rock music is a type of loud, modern music. *Rock* bands usually have *lead* and *bass* guitars, a singer and a *drummer*.

royal (adj.)
of or about a king or queen or their family

rumour (n.)
something that a lot of people talk about but that may not be true

satellite (adj.)
Satellites are sent into space to send pictures and information to Earth. *Satellite* TV is broadcast using a *satellite*.

sexuality (n.)
A person's *sexuality* tells you if they prefer to have sex with men, women, both or neither.

single (n.)
a CD or *record* that has only one song

stadium (n.)
a large place with many seats used for football matches, for example

star (n.)
a very famous singer, *musician* or actor

station (n.)
a radio or television company

studio (n.)
a special room where television or radio shows are made, or where people record music

support (v.)
to care for someone by giving them money, food or clothes, for example; to agree with a person or idea

talented (adj.)
A *talented* person can do something very well.

teenager (n.)
a person who is between 13 and 19 years old

tour (n.)
When a band, singer or *musician* go on a *tour*, they travel to a lot of different places to *perform*.

Western (adj.)
in or from North America or the countries in the west of Europe

References

Some of the sentences in this book have been taken from other books, magazines and films. Each of those sentences in this book has a number after it. Those numbers appear below, with information about which book, magazine or film the sentence came from.

[1] *Freddie Mercury: The Untold Story* (Arte France; DoRo Produktion; Zweites Deutsches Fernsehen, 2000)
[2] https://www.mirror.co.uk/film/inside-mary-austin-freddie-mercurys-13474118
[3] *Freddie Mercury: The Untold Story*
[4] Richards, M. and Langthorne, M., *Somebody to Love* (Blink Publishing, 2009), page 102
[5] Sheffield, N., *Life on Two Legs* (Trident Management Ltd, 2013), chapter 12
[6] Brooks, G. and Lupton, S., ed., *Freddie Mercury: A Life, In His Own Words* (Mercury Songs Ltd, 2006), page 48
[7] *Queen: Days of our Lives* (Globe Productions; British Broadcasting Company, 2011)
[8] *Queen: Days of our Lives*
[9] *Queen: Days of our Lives*
[10] Thomas, D., *Mojo: Their Britannic Majesties Request*, (Emap, Issue 69, August 1999)
[11] Hutton, J. and Wapshott, T., *Mercury and Me* (Bloomsbury Publishing, 1995), page 2
[12] *Mercury and Me*, page 6
[13] *Mercury and Me*, page 16
[14] *Mercury and Me*, page 21
[15] *Mercury and Me*, page 72
[16] *The Great Pretender* (Eagle Rock; Mercury Songs Ltd, 2012)
[17] *Mercury and Me*, page 82
[18] *Somebody to Love*, pages 363-4

Bibliography

Books
- Richards, M. and Langthorne, M., *Somebody to Love*, Blink Publishing, London, 2009
- Sheffield, N., *Life on Two Legs*, Trident Management Ltd, London, 2013
- Brooks, G. and Lupton, S., ed., *Freddie Mercury: A Life, In His Own Words* (Mercury Songs Ltd, 2006)
- Hutton, J. and Wapshott, T., *Mercury and Me*, Bloomsbury Publishing, London, 1995

Films
- *Freddie Mercury: The Untold Story* (Arte France; DoRo Produktion; Zweites Deutsches Fernsehen, 2000)
- *Queen: Days of our Lives* (Globe Productions; British Broadcasting Company, 2011)
- *The Great Pretender* (Eagle Rock; Mercury Songs Ltd, 2012)